THE 7 PRINCIPLES TO MANIFESTING IN ABUNDANCE

Dr. Minniel Douglas

ISBN: 978-1-7366874-0-6

For permission requests, contact: Minniel Douglas at minniel@peacebeloved.co

This book is for informational purposes only. It is not to give professional advice or
assistance. It is not to replace or provide mental health treatment or diagnosis.

First Edition 2021
Printed in USA

www.peacebeloved.co

To my Beloveds,
my Husband, my Daughter, my Son, and my Mommie, I
love you all forever and always. You each teach me what it
means to love God, myself, and people, on a daily basis. I
would not be who I am without you. Thank you for your
patience and support along this journey. XOXO

TABLE OF CONTENTS

PREFACE

This book is a journal. This book is a devotional. This book will help you set the foundation for Manifesting in Abundance through our seven foundational Manifesting principles.

We all want to have Abundance, but do we know what Abundance is. We talk about Manifesting things in our lives, but can we honestly say we know what it means to manifest anything. Before we discuss the principles of Manifesting, let us look at the definitions of Manifesting and Abundance.

By definition, Manifesting is to make something readily perceived by the eye or the understanding; to make evident or apparent. Therefore, when you state that you are Manifesting something, you make something visible to the world and yourself. You will be able to see that thing with your eyes, and others will be able to see it as well. When you manifest something, it is no longer a thought in your head or a dream you are saying you want to achieve. It is something that is happening, something that everyone can see.

Now that we understand manifesting let us talk about Abundance. Abundance, by definition, is an extremely plentiful or over sufficient quantity or supply. It is an overflowing fullness. Therefore, Abundance is not just enough of something. Abundance is where you have enough for you and enough for those around you. You have what you need and want and still have more to go around.

We need to pause here and deal with the idea that Abundance is only for the material world or is only about how much you have, be it a thing or money or both. Abundance can be about money and things, but the most incredible Abundance you can have is in the spiritual world. God does not only want to bless us in Abundance in the flesh but the Spirit. This journey is about understanding that true Abundance begins with the Abundance that comes from walking in a relationship with God. As we walk in a relationship with God, we learn more about who He is and who we are, and what our limits are. This way, when God gives us the Vision that is beyond us and our capacity, we know that Abundance is possible. After all, the Bible says, "greater is He that is in me than he that is in the world." It also says, "I can do all things through Christ who strengthens me." We know this not just because we read it, but because we walk in this place of truth, as we walk with God.

Understanding the basics of Manifesting and Abundance allows us to get to the definition that is so crucial in this book. What is Manifesting in Abundance? *Manifesting in Abundance is overflowing and overly sufficient supply that is plain to see with the eyes and easily understood with the mind.* Manifesting in Abundance is seeing the Vision flourish and then flourish to a greater place than you ever dreamed. For instance, you decide the Vision is to own a vending machine company that makes about $200,000 annually. Since you set the foundation and live the principles of Manifesting in Abundance, not only do you make $200,000 annually, but you also make an extra $500,000, and your business is now in multiple cities and with numerous employees. How does this work, you ask? Let's find out.

Disclaimer: it is essential to note that this book will not give specific steps to take your business from here to here or steps on how to change your relationship. This book is going to help you with setting the foundation for manifesting. Therefore, no matter what you want to manifest, you know where to start. Also, if at any point in reading and working through this book, you feel like you need some professional help from a counselor, advisor, pastor, or Life coach, please get that help. This book is not to take the place of professional assistance in any way.

Also, we suggest that you grab some spare paper or a journal just in case you need extra space to write down your answers or any revelations that you receive while you go through this journey.

With all of that said, Let's begin Manifesting in Abundance!!!

CHAPTER 1

Get Ready!

Setting a Prayerful Intention

To start this journey of Manifesting in Abundance, you have to set a Prayerful Intention. A Prayerful Intention is setting a goal that has been selected by you and God. It's making a goal with God's purpose in mind. This type of intention allows you to link up with God so that you move when He moves. It enables you to figure out what is the goal of this journey of Manifesting in Abundance. What am I supposed to be Manifesting, and where is God leading me right now, at this moment?

Take a moment right now and be still. Connect with your thoughts and emotions, and then connect with God. You want to take this time to evaluate what should be your Prayerful Intention for this time in your life. Asking yourself, what should be your goal right now? You may have thoughts, but since we are trying to set a Prayerful Intention, make sure to ask God what His thoughts are. One of the best ways to manifest in Abundance is to make sure that what you intend to manifest is in line with what God plans to manifest in your life. The best way to find out His plan is to ask. So, take this moment, you and God, and make a Prayerful intention.

After you have spoken with yourself and God, please answer the following in as much detail as you can:

What is your Prayerful Intention for this time? (It is important not to move forward until you get an intention so that you and God are on the same page for the time)

Did God give you more information? Did He give you a whole Vision? If so, what is it?

What do you think about this Prayerful Intention?

How do you feel about the Prayerful Intention? Are you happy? Are there any concerns? If so what are they?

Now that you have identified your Prayerful Intention and examined your thoughts and feelings, it is time to release. So, take a moment to release anything that will hinder you from Manifesting this Prayerful Intention. Release anything that may concern you unto God, for Him to answer and resolve, or just for Him to hold and not you. The truth is, if God says that you are to manifest something, then you will manifest that thing. You do not want to be the shadow that blocks the manifestation from becoming visible or the wall that blocks the manifestation from reaching Abundance.

CHAPTER 2

Get Set!!

We have the intention. Now it is time to get set for the 7 Principles of Manifesting in Abundance. Getting set has a lot to do with understanding Mindfulness, Inner Mindfulness, and Spiritual Mindfulness. Let's begin.

Mindfulness is a practice that causes you to be still and pay attention to the things going on around you in great detail, from the trees outside to the air on your arms from the fan blowing on you to the different colors on your TV or computer screen. With Mindfulness, you are learning to focus by becoming aware of the things around you in greater detail. When you focus on something in detail, you can eventually get to the place of a clear mind and began to meditate.

My business is called Peace, Beloved. It is the sanctuary for medivotion. Medivotion is a unique process that merges meditation and devotion. You can find the full definition at the end of this book and find more information on the Peace, Beloved website, peace-beloved.co. At any rate, at Peace, Beloved, we practice a unique kind of Mindfulness, Mindfulness that focuses on the outside world and the inside and spiritual world. These other types of mindfulness practices we call Inner Mindfulness and Spiritual Mindfulness, respectively.

Inner Mindfulness focuses on assessing the things happening within you and assessing your inner feelings, thoughts, intentions, goals, etc. You consider all of this to deal with them, make plans on how to be better or accomplish a thing, or release those things you have assessed and move forward. Inner Mindfulness looks at the things that you keep hidden from others and sometimes even yourself. It is taking a moment to examine you, the real you, even the parts of you that others may not think is okay or that you may not think is okay. The completed assessments ensure that you know things that need to change in your life and change those things. Now, this is not to take the place of professional therapy if it is required. Inner Mindfulness is to help you do self-evaluation and self-work. Even while doing this, if you find that professional help is needed, that is okay. Seek it out. Your self-work makes you even more ready to receive what the professional has to offer you.

The other type of Mindfulness is called Spiritual Mindfulness. Mindfulness and Inner Mindfulness focuses on what's around you and in you, but Spiritual Mindfulness focuses explicitly on God's presence around and in you. Spiritual Mindfulness assesses what is happening in the Spirit. How God is shifting what He is doing in you and in your environment. This leads to a place where God can speak to you and give you directions.

Let's check-in. In your own words, explain the following:

Mindfulness:

_____

_____

_____

Inner Mindfulness:

_____

_____

_____

Spiritual Mindfulness:

_____
_____
_____

Understanding Mindfulness, Inner Mindfulness, and Spiritual Mindfulness will effectively help you do the 7 principles of Manifesting in Abundance. Each principle can get as deep or as shallow as you would like. Knowing what is happening physically and spiritually in you and around you, allows you to grow closer to yourself and God.

Let me remind you, this book is not going to give steps on how to take your business from here to here or how to change your relationship, Peace, Beloved does offer Life Coaching for that. This book helps you have the foundation so that no matter what the intention is, you know where to start. Because no matter what you are trying to manifest, you always start the same, and you always need to remember the 7 Principles for Manifesting in Abundance. It's time. Let's learn the principles!

CHAPTER 3

Go!!!

Principle 1: Being in the Moment

We live lives where there is always something that needs to be done or something that needs to be tended to. We tend to spend our days going from one responsibility to the next, all while taking care of some business or social activity on our phones or tablets. Multi-tasking is what we do, every day and all day. It is our way of life. The problem with this is, we are never truly in any one moment. We can be on vacation but spend so much time posting pictures to Instagram, tweeting about events, and writing stories to Facebook, that we never really stop and just enjoy the vacation.

The first time that I experienced this concept, I was at a meeting at work. It was late, and everyone had somewhere else they wanted to be, which was quite evident. We were all on our phones doing something completely different from Instagram to Facebook, to talking to someone on the phone to texting. My manager came in and made us all put our phones away, and then she made one plea. She said, "For the next 30 mins I just need you guys to be here now. Have your mind and body here now. If you can do that for me, we can finish quickly."

This made me think what would happen if on the regular I practice this idea of being here now, not just in body but mind and spirit too. Before we go any further let me ask you a question. When was the last time you truly just stopped? I am not talking about when you laid down to go to sleep. I am talking about during the day.

When was the last time you stopped?

_____

_____

_____

What caused you to stop?

_____

_____

_____

Being in the Moment has a lot to do with being still, being mindful, being inner and spiritually mindful, and being here now. Something is taking place in every moment, something that is good, something that is uncertain, something that makes you feel something and something where God is. Being in the Moment means I stop moving and assess around me physically, assess spiritually, and assess within me. I can evaluate one of these areas or all of these areas depending on how much time I have. Being in the Moment means that I am literally in the moment.

Learning to really be still and pay attention to what is going on in this particular moment is an easy concept to understand, but sometimes it is hard to do. After all, as we said, we are people that live lives that multi-task all day and every day. The challenge is to take each moment as it comes because it is a moment you will not get back. Take each experience as it arrives, for it is an experience you will not experience precisely like that ever again. Are you ready to start living your life where every now and then, at least once throughout the day, you are stopping and truly Being in the Moment?

Being in the Moment can be brief, or it can be a long moment, that is all dependent on where you are and how much time you would like to offer up. The below is for a moment that is roughly

5 mins or so. It is a moment to assess your outside and inner world. During this moment, please do not use any electronic devices unless the device is what you are using to read this book. Let's begin. Take a moment to center (quiet and still) yourself by taking some deep breaths. Take the breaths in through your nose and out through your mouth. Do it again, in through your nose and out through your mouth. Continue to do this style of breathing slowly 5 times or as many times as you need to be still and really be where you are.

Now that you are centered, please answer these questions in as much detail as you can (the detail slows you down and allows you to focus):

What do you see right in front of you?
_____
_____
_____
_____
_____

What color is it?
_____
_____
_____

Is it more than one color? If so, what are the colors?
_____
_____
_____

What textures do you see on it? Is it rough or smooth? Soft or hard?

_____
_____
_____

How does this thing make you feel?

_____
_____
_____

How does stopping and looking at this thing in so much detail make you feel?

_____
_____
_____

Now close your eyes and feel the room. What does the room feel like cold, warm, etc....?

_____
_____
_____

Is there extra air coming into your space from somewhere, like a fan or something? Do you like this extra air at this moment while you are being still, why or why not?

_____
_____
_____

Now smell the room, what does it smell like? Be specific.

_____
_____
_____

Do you like the smell or do you want to change it?

_____

_____

_____

Again, take some deep breaths, in through your nose and out through your mouth. We will switch from assessing the physical and inner world to evaluating the spiritual and inner one. This will again be about 5 mins depending on God. When you evaluate the spiritual world, you are feeling with your spirit-man for the presence of God. We are not looking for anything else, just God's presence. The truth is God is always present and ready to help and comfort. The other truth is that God is within you as a believer. Your spirit-man is always in search of Him. We tend to be so busy that we miss His presence daily. So, taking the time to be in the moment will really help you feel God's presence and then hear God throughout the day because He is always there.

Again, take the time to take some deep breaths. Center yourself and begin to feel the room around you. Allow yourself to pray and ask God to allow you to feel His presence. When you believe you feel Him near, answer these questions:

How do you feel in this moment?

_____

_____

_____

Can you feel God's presence in this moment?

_____

_____

_____

What does His presence feel like to you (be as detailed as you can)?

_____
_____
_____

Are you ok with just sitting in His presence? Why or why not?

_____
_____
_____

Does His presence make you want to leave or stay? Why or why not?

_____
_____
_____

Sit in that moment as long as you want to. There is no rush to get through the moment or to move on. There is a healing of your mind, body, and Spirit in the presence of God. So please spend as long as you and God want to spend in the moment.

As you move through that moment, take another assessment. Ask yourself, has God spoken? If so, answer these questions:

What did God say?

_____
_____
_____
_____
_____

What does He want you to do?

_____
_____
_____

Is He happy with where you are on your journey of life?

_____
_____
_____

Now that God has spoken, how do you feel about the moment?

_____
_____
_____

Are you energized or drained?

_____
_____
_____

Do you feel ready for what's next, like the rest of your day or bedtime?

_____
_____
_____

Like we stated, Being in the Moment can be a long moment or a short moment. It is all up to you. The above was the moment you might take at the beginning of the day, at lunch or bedtime, basically, during a time when you have time to really listen to God and sit with Him. A brief moment can really just be the first part or the second part of the moments described above. The idea with the brief moment is really just stopping breathing and assessing what is going on around you, or in you, or spiritually. Let's try a brief moment.

Take some deep breaths, in through your nose and out through your mouth. Allow yourself to be still, right here. Now assess what is around you:

Where are you?

_____

_____

_____

How does this space feel to you?

_____

_____

_____

What do you see that you like?

_____

_____

_____

Now really be mindful of that thing you like, what are the colors?

_____

_____

_____

What does it feel like?

_____

_____

How do you feel looking at it?

Now really center yourself, take some deep breaths, find a happy feeling, inhale the calm, and exhale any anxiety. Keep doing this breathing of inhaling calm and exhaling anxiety until you feel the calm. Congratulations, you have just had a brief moment.

Remember, Being in the Moment can look like taking a step back, taking some deep breaths, putting all of your devices down, and just being where you are. Focusing all of your attention, spiritually, mentally, and physically right in that moment. However, you choose to practice Being in the Moment, it will help you to live a more abundant life because you will become more and more aware of the things that God has already placed around and within you. Therefore, they are visible to you, which means they are manifested to you. Now, you will be able to know when they have become more than just enough. You will know when they have become abundant because you are aware of them, and they are manifested in your life. Regularly, take some time to practice Being in the Moment.

CHAPTER 4

Principle 2: Walking in Truth

We now understand what Being in the Moment means, to really be right here and right now physically, mentally, emotionally, and spiritually. We are going to take this idea a step further. Let us start with you taking the time to assess yourself and your situation. Say a quick prayer or enter into a meditation space and ask God to help you see the more in-depth picture of you and your situation. Then answer the following:

What do I think about me? How do I feel about me?

_____
_____
_____

What are my boundaries in relationships, at work, at home? Do I enforce my boundaries? Why or why not?

_____
_____
_____

What do I think about where I am in life? Have I accomplished my goals or am on the road to accomplishing my goals?

_____
_____
_____

What do I think about the relationships I am in? How do I

feel about these relationships? Boyfriend or girlfriend? Parents? Spouse? Children? Friends?

_____
_____
_____

Are my relationships edifying to me? Am I edifying to them? Are we helping each other to be better?

_____
_____
_____

What is my current overall situation? What do I think about it?

_____
_____
_____
_____
_____

Lastly how would I describe my relationship with God? What do I think about that? How should it be different?

_____
_____
_____

You have taken a moment to not just be in the moment and assess what is going on, but you have dug a little deeper into your whole situation. Please really evaluate if something else weighs on your mind that is part of you or your situation that you need to dig deeper into. If so, write it here.

_____
_____
_____

By taking a more in-depth look at you and your situation, you know your truth. You know the reality about where you are and what you think about where you are. Now we are ready for Principle 2: Walking in Truth. Walking in Truth is about owning your truth and about asking yourself, does something need to be done to change my truth, or is my truth good as is? When you decide that something needs to change about your truth, Walking in Truth also says to take action about it. At the same time, if you looked at your truth and you said it was good as is, Walking in Truth says to be grateful for where you are and live contently and with joy. So, let's find out. Read all of your answers from above and say a quick prayer for guidance. And then answer the following:

Am I content with my truth? Why or Why not?

_____
_____
_____

Can I honestly look at my reality and say I am where I am supposed to be right now?

_____
_____
_____

Does something about my truth need to change?

_____
_____
_____

If so, what?

_____
_____
_____

If no, am I walking contently daily?

_____
_____
_____

Is there a struggle or something weighing on me?

_____
_____
_____

Is there joy or something lifting me?

_____
_____
_____

If your above answers say that you are content and happy with where you are and live in that comfortable and joyous space daily, I am truly happy for you and encourage you to continue to live in that space and continue to walk in the truth of that space. Please make sure you daily thank God for being in that kind of space in this season of life, for it is truly a blessing. Walking in Truth says I am content with where I am, and I am walking grateful for this time in my life right now.

If your above answers say that you are okay with where you are, and you do not live in a happy space daily. I urge you to fully acknowledge that truth and then really take some time in meditation to figure out what is stopping you from living in a happy space. For instance:

What weighs on you?

_____

_____

_____

What burdens you?

_____

_____

_____

What robs you of your peace?

_____

_____

_____

Once you realize what things are causing you not to live a happy and joyous life, you can really begin to Walk in Truth. I mean, you can start to make intentional changes to get rid of those things that do not bring you joy or rearrange how you think about those things so that they are no longer burdens and weights for you. Sometimes we find that the things that we believe are weighing us down are actually teaching us about ourselves and helping to build us up. Because we eventually realize that by dealing with that weight, we are more and more equipped for what is going on around us and in us. In this situation, Walking in Truth says I am okay with where I am, but I am not okay with my daily feelings and processes, and I am ready to do something about that Now.

If you answered the above questions and realized you are not content with where you are and want things to change, it is time to Walk in Truth. This means admitting that I am not okay with my current situation or my current feelings about my situation, and I am ready to make a change. Walking in Truth here is really about doing the work that will change your truth. If that means you need to seek professional assistance, then do so. If that means you start doing more self-care methods, then do so. One of the greatest self-care methods you can practice is medivotion because it helps you know yourself and know God. The more we grow in relationship with God, the more we grow in relationship with us, and the more we can live in the wisdom that comes from God's revelation. In this situation, Walking in Truth says I am not happy with where I am, and I am changing it Now.

What is your truth right now?

_____
_____
_____

Does something need to change? If so, what?

_____
_____
_____
_____
_____

Are you going to make the change if something is needed?

_____
_____
_____

Are you Walking in Truth? If not, are you ready to change that?

_____
_____
_____

Know that at some point in our lives, we all experience one of these three scenarios. This is why it is essential to follow these principles because we need to continuously be aware of our moments and where we really are, walk in truth, and know when a change needs to occur around and in us.

CHAPTER 5

Principle 3: Walking with God

Now that we have been in the moment and taken it more in-depth and are walking in truth, we are ready for Walking with God. God explained it to me like this: To manifest in Abundance, it requires us to spend time with God and grow in God. Only when we do this can we truly walk in our purpose, understand purpose and self, and genuinely Manifest in Abundance.

The ultimate thing to manifest is purpose. In every season in our lives, there is a purpose. Honestly, sometimes what is destined to be accomplished in that season is not what you intended to accomplish at all. This is why it is so vital to set Prayerful Intentions. Remember, Prayerful Intentions allow us to connect with God so that we can be sure that the intention, the purpose, for this time is not just what we want but also what He wants.

To truly Manifest in Abundance, we have to walk with God. That means we have to spend time with God. We need to sit in His presence. We need to hear what He is saying, and we need to read His Word. Walking with God is not about being a scripture quoter or going to church all the time. Walking with God is about being in a relationship with the Creator of the universe, the Savior of our souls. It's about being connected to the Source of all things. When we stay connected to Him, we get peace, understanding about Him, and understanding about us. Since God created you and me, He understands us in ways that we do not even know ourselves. He is then able to explain us to us in a way that makes sense to us. God can explain purpose in a way that may not have even crossed your mind yet. He knows what you can really accomplish. He knows that you can, and you will Manifest in Abundance.

All that being said, let's start this Walking with God. Answer the following.

Do you know God?

_____
_____
_____

What does knowing God mean to you?

_____
_____
_____
_____
_____

Do you already have a relationship with God? If so, what does it look like? Is it a good relationship or a bad one? Explain.

_____
_____
_____

Do you know Jesus? What does knowing Him mean to you?

_____
_____
_____

Are you in relationship with Jesus? If so, what does that look like?

_____
_____
_____

Is being in a relationship with God the same as being in a relationship with Jesus? How or How not?

_____

_____

_____

Some may say why did I word the questions this way. We need to understand that some know God but not Jesus. This being said, this author's view is that the only way to be in a relationship with God and have a one-on-one conversation with God is through Jesus Christ. Jesus came, and He died and rose again in order so that we could once again be children of God. If you do not know Jesus Christ as your Savior and you would like more information, or you would like to accept Him as Savior, please contact us through the information at the back of the book.

All this being said, to Walk with God all you need to start is a willing heart. Let's answer the following:

When was the last time you spent time with God alone, meaning without being in church or at a church function (including streaming it)?

_____

_____

_____

The last time you were alone with God, why did you spend time with God?

_____

_____

_____

Did you find the time helpful? Why or why not?

_____

_____

_____

What did you use to spend time with God, like a Bible, devotional, music, you, etc....?

_____

_____

_____

Do you always use the same thing? Why or Why not?

_____

_____

_____

How would you rate your relationship within God, where 1 is we do not talk, and 10 is we talk all the time, and I am close to him?

_____

_____

_____

Are you ok with this rating? Would you prefer things to be different between you and God?

_____

_____

_____

Do you want that true abundance that comes only from Walking with God? Why or Why not?

_____

_____

_____

Take a moment and reread your answers. Understand time alone with God does not have to belong. If you are ready and willing to grow in a relationship with God, there are many ways to start. One of the easiest ways to start growing in relationship with God in prayer. Literally, just talking to God and asking Him to come to sit with you during meditation or medication, asking Him to allow you to feel the peace that comes from His presence. You can also use this book and really take the time to do each prayer. You can do a medivotion session at Peace, Beloved individually, or in a general session to help you grow in your relationship with God. You can use other devotional books. You can go to church. You can talk to other believers in Christ. To grow in a relationship with God, you do not have to do all these things, but you need to do something because Manifesting in Abundance requires you to walk with God and grow in a relationship with Him. Only when you walk with God and grow in a relationship with God that you know and understand purpose and yourself. When you walk with God, you turn from solely looking at the truth in your situation to what the Abundance in the situation could be. You begin to see the greater that may lay ahead that you were not able to see before. You stop looking at what appears to be your truth, and instead, you see God's truth about your situation. To state that another way, when you walk in relationship with God, you begin to walk in truth through the lens of God, seeing what He sees, seeing the victory that He has already walked out for you.

It is truly our prayer that your relationship with God grows tremendously through this process, that He allows you to feel His presence, understand your purpose, and understand yourself. We pray that God will do something truly extraordinary in your life and that you will genuinely Manifest in Abundance. In Jesus name Amen. Peace, Beloved.

CHAPTER 6

Principle 4: Enjoying the Moment

Congratulations, we are at the halfway mark!!! You have done an excellent job on all the work you have put in so far. Know that as you practice these principles, they become more manageable and become a part of your daily journey of life. This way, you can genuinely Manifest in Abundance regardless of the intention. Since we are halfway, let us recap. We have talked about Principle 1: Being in the Moment, which means really means be right there in that moment, in that space. Then we talked about Principle 2: Walking in Truth, really examining where we are and the truth about that, whether we want to move from that space or be content in that space. Lastly, we have talked about Principle 3: Walking with God, really growing in relationship with God, and spending time with Him.

Now we are on Principle 4: Enjoying the Moment. In this principle, we will take a step back and revisit Principle 1: Being in the Moment, because we need to first be in the moment before we can really enjoy the moment. Answer the following questions as truthfully as possible.

When you practiced Being in the Moment, did you spend more time examining the things you did not like about the moment, the things you did like about the moment, or were they neutral (things you did not necessarily like or dislike)?

_____
_____
_____

When you go into or through a situation, do you spend more time looking at the positive things happening or the negative things happening?

On a regular day, are you seeing all the wrong things or all the right things?

When you regularly look at your thoughts, are you thinking sad, happy, negative, or positive thoughts?

Lastly, are you a glass half full or a glass half empty kind of person?

When you look at your above answers, are there more answers saying you consider the positive or the negative around you?

Thank you for answering truthfully. Most of us spend more time thinking about all the things we wish were different around us. We spend a lot of time thinking about all the things that we are not happy with that are happening around us versus looking at all the things we are satisfied with. Most people have the grass is greener on the other side kind of mentality. It always seems that other people have it better. It is the reason why we spend so much time on Instagram and Facebook, checking out what other people are doing. We tend to feel like something else could be going on in our lives that would be better than what is currently going on. When truthfully, many amazing things are going on around you and in you right now. God is doing some mind-blowing things in your life right now. Even the fact that you are doing this guide is a testament to that. Of course, there are times that we want things to be different or things to change, but even in those times, there is at least one positive thing happening around us. All we need to do is take a moment and look. Also, it goes without saying, the grass is not greener on the other side. Everyone has their own issues to work through. They just might not be the same issues that you are working through.

This chapter is about taking a moment not to just be in the moment, but to really enjoy the moment that you are in right now. Let's do the following. Before you do, please be patient with yourself during this set of questions. As always, please be as honest as you can. I want you to take some time getting into the moment. If you need to go back to Chapter 3 and use the exercise we did for Being in the Moment, please do. If you do not need to go back and you can get into this moment right here on your own, that is awesome too. Remember, the more you practice, the easier it will become. Once you find yourself truly immersed in this moment right here, answer the following questions, trying to focus only on positive things in detail:

What is going on around you?

_____

_____

_____

Is this positive thing always present?

Did you notice it before?

If not, what did you see before?

Why do you think you saw the other thing instead of the positive thing the first time?

If you did see the positive thing before, is it different now or the same?

What around you makes you happy? Explain.

_____
_____

What, in this moment right now, is bringing you happiness?
_____
_____
_____

What are you grateful for right now?
_____
_____
_____

What do you think would happen within you if you spent the next 5 mins just sitting in a place of gratitude and allowing yourself to enjoy what is in front of you?
_____
_____
_____
_____
_____

Put on a timer for 5 minutes. For the next 5 minutes, honestly sit in a space or mindset of gratitude, being thankful for that thing or a person you are happy to have or be experiencing in this moment. Ready, set, Go.

Now that the 5 minutes is up, how do you feel?
_____
_____
_____

How does your mind feel? What kind of thoughts are you having?
_____

_____
_____

How does your body feel?

_____
_____
_____

How does your heart feel?

_____
_____
_____
_____
_____

Overall are you better now that you have spent 5 minutes enjoying this moment than before you took the 5 minutes? Why or why not?

_____
_____
_____

The more time you spend Enjoying the Moment, the easier it becomes to enjoy the moment. You can begin living, enjoying the positive things that happen all around you daily. The things that sometimes get overshadowed by the problems and issues and that arise throughout the day. Please take a moment to enjoy your moments. Being mindful of the good and God all around you.

CHAPTER 7

Principle 5: Trusting God without Limits

We are going to pause. Please take a moment and fortify your hearts and souls. This chapter is really about taking some boundaries off so that you can get to the place of Abundance you seek. Be open and prayerful. We are headed to manifested Abundance.

We will start by explaining you are limitless before we talk about trusting God without limits. This is because you need to understand that trusting God without limits needs to be connected to you. It is not enough to say God has no limits, but you do not see how that applies to you in its totality.

Let's Go, Beloved.

Trusting God without limits. Limitless. We have talked about walking in a relationship with God and how important it is to grow in a relationship with God, but we are about to take that to another level. See, our relationship with God does not just give us information about God and who He is, and what He does. Our relationship with God provides a deeper connection to God. It provides the link to who God is. God is not looking to just show you who He is. He wants to be connected to your inmost part. God wants you to be so familiar with Him, you can feel His presence all the time. He wants to be in an intimate relationship with you. God wants to be the vine and you the branches so that He can provide you the nutrients and love you need to live and thrive in life. He wants to be your vine and you the branches so you can produce fruit in Abundance. The truth is, when we are connected with God in this way, we understand not only does God have no limits, but we also are without limits. The Bible tells us that Christ is in us, and Christ is in God, and God is therefore within us too. This means not only are we connected to God and Jesus but the very Creator of the universe, the very sustainer of our souls, is within us. Pause. Breathe. We have said a lot. Take a moment and let that digest, and then when you are ready, answer the following questions:

How do you feel about what you just read?

What does it mean to you that the very Creator, the Great I AM, lives within you?

What do you think about the kind of relationship that God is trying to build with you?

Do you want that same kind of relationship with Him that He wants with you? Why?

Limitless. The Bible says I can do all things through Christ who strengthens me. It also says that everything that God says will come to pass because He is not a man that He should lie. The Bible also teaches that God is so vast in all His God-ness that no one name can completely encompass Him. God is simply I AM. So, if I AM lives in me, and He is who I am connected to, then is it not possible that I can do exceedingly abundantly above anything that I can think or imagine? If I am connected to God, and therefore in a relationship with God, I learn that He can do anything but fail. I understand this because as I grow in a relationship with Him, I see Him changing things in my life. He begins to change my situation. God begins to show me myself. He shows me my great points and my bad. He helps me change and become better. Then at some point, I look up, and I know myself better than I ever have before. All because the one who made me explained to me myself.

Beloved, God does not have the limits of time because He works at His own time. He does not have the limitations of resources because He owns the universe. God does not have the limits of what other people say because He is greater than any person or god. It has been tested and proven. So, if God has no limits and He lives in you, then you do not have limits either. You are limitless.

Please reread this information again and really think and pray about it. You must understand that you are limitless when you are connected to God. There are no limits because when we are connected to God, and in a relationship with Him, we begin to want what He wants for our lives. We begin to set Prayerful Intentions, which are in line with God's will and destiny for our lives. The limitless place that comes from being connected to God comes because His promises are yes and Amen. When we live connected to God, we begin to manifest His promises in our lives. So yes, Beloved, you are limitless. Pause. Breathe. Answer these questions:

What promises from God in your life have you put limits on?

How does the knowledge that you are limitless when you are connected to God make you feel? How does it make you think?

What about your life should change with the knowledge that you are limitless?

What about your mentality should change with the knowledge that you are limitless?

If God is limitless and you are too, should you be able to trust Him without putting limits on Him? Explain?

The more we grow in an intimate relationship with God, the more we understand not only His power and limitless-ness but ours as well. The more we also trust God. We tend to put the same limits we put on ourselves on God. Now that we understand the limitations we put on ourselves from us, from family, society, etc..... do not need to exist in our lives because we are limitless in Christ; we can also accept that God can be trusted without limits. God does not lie to us. He does not promise one thing and does not deliver. God is always there, and God always does as He says. God is trustworthy, and He is limitless. Therefore, we can trust Him without limits. Answer the following.

Do you trust God? Why or why not?

_____
_____
_____

(If the answer was no, we pray that you take a moment and pray and really talk to God about why you do not trust Him and ask Him to show you that you can trust Him. Please take a moment to pray before moving forward)

Since you trust God, do you believe that He is limitless? Why or why not?

_____
_____
_____

Do you believe it is possible to trust God without limits since you are limitless because of Him? Why or why not?

_____
_____
_____

Is God worthy enough to be trusted without limits? Why or why not?

_____
_____
_____

Do you trust God without limits? (Be Honest)

_____

_____

_____

God, we pray that you help us trust you without limits, to truly see that you are limitless and trustworthy. We pray that you help us understand and accept that we are limitless because we are connected to you. Help us grow more and more intimate with you so that we are so connected, we can say you are our vine, and we are your branches, and we bear fruit for you. God help us to accept your truths. In Jesus name, Amen.

This is our prayer for you and for us. We genuinely believe this is a journey, and the more we try, the better we become. If you find yourself a little uneasy or confused about this chapter, please take a moment and go back to the beginning of the chapter and reread it. If you need to see the video about this chapter, please go to peacebeloved.co. Take as much time as you need to grasp this topic and for it to resonate with you. Remember, all of the principles for Manifesting in Abundance go together, and it is important to trust God without limits to produce Abundance. Abundance means an over-sufficient supply; therefore, Abundance is really a limitless state of being.

Peace, Beloved, we are ready for the next principle.

CHAPTER 8

Principle 6: Vision

The dictionary says Vision means the act or power of anticipating that which will or may come to be or the act or power of sensing with eyes. For us to really manifest in Abundance, we need vision. We need to be able to anticipate and see our goals. We started this book by talking about Prayerful Intentions. Honestly, sitting down and praying and making an intention with God's purpose in mind. We started the book there because we need to know the intention we are working on and see the vision for this point in our lives. Vision allows us to know the intention, and when we have met the intention and surpass the intention. Abundance is about reaching the intention and then surpassing it. After all, Abundance is an over-sufficient supply of something. Therefore, we are not just trying to accomplish the Prayerful Intention. We want to surpass that intention. We want the whole vision God has for us.

Now, please answer the following:

What was your Prayerful Intention at the beginning of this book? (It is okay if you need to look back to chapter 1, that is what this section is for)

_____
_____
_____

Take a moment and pray, does anything need to be added to that intention? If so, what?

_____

_____

_____

Have you reached your Prayerful Intention? If not, what parts are still missing, and what needs to be done from here?

_____

_____

_____

If you added to your intention, is there anything you need to change about what you are doing in order to reach that intention, now?

_____

_____

_____

Have you surpassed your intention? Have you made it to abundance? Why or why not?

_____

_____

_____

_____

_____

Are you worried about anything pertaining to this intention?

_____

_____

_____

No matter where you are on your Prayerful Intention journey, do not worry. I am sure that there is something about your Prayerful

Intention beyond you, something that is outside of your comfort zone, and that is okay. If you are wondering how I know, it is because it is a Prayerful Intention. A Prayerful Intention means you sought God on the purpose for the season, and God is really good at giving us an intention that we were made to do but that we need connection with Him to complete. The reason for this is because God wants us. He wants us to grow in a closer relationship with Him and begin to trust Him without limits, and to know that our connectedness to Him makes us limitless as well. The key to all this is the connectedness to God. God knows that the Prayerful Intention takes you and Him, not just you. Therefore, that discomfort you feel is intentional from God. Remember, Vision says I will complete the intention and surpass the intention and manifest in Abundance. Vision says that God told me the Prayerful Intention, and I believe Him. I believe that He has no limits, and I trust that I am limitless because He lives in me. Therefore, no matter what is happening around me, I chose to see the Vision of my Prayerful Intention.

Please answer the following:

Beloved, do you have Vision? Can you see the Prayerful Intention, see it surpassed, and manifested in Abundance?

_____
_____
_____

Can you see the intention and beyond it in your mind's eye?

_____
_____
_____

Can you trust God for the Abundance?

_____
_____

Can you see that to complete the Prayerful Intention, you need you and God?

Can you begin to work like this requires you and God, not just you and your thoughts and knowledge?

Beloved, truly we are almost there. Keep practicing the principles and hold on to Vision. Work with God, and you can indeed Manifest in Abundance.

CHAPTER 9

Principle 7: Being Careful with What You Say

Have you ever heard; you can have what you say? If you say you can, you will. If you say you can't, then you won't. Or have you heard that there is life and death in the power of the tongue? We truly can have what we say, which is why it is so crucial for us to be careful about what we say.

Now that we have taken the time to know what Prayerful Intention is and set Vision. We must pray that intention and speak that intention into our lives every day. When we do this, we remind God about what He said He would do (not that God really needs the reminder) and remind ourselves about what God said He would do daily. This way, as we go through the days, weeks, the months, or the years with this particular intention, we know precisely the Prayerful Intention that God set for this time. We can walk knowing exactly where we are going and what we are trying to accomplish. And yes, some intentions take a little longer to manifest than others but understand everything manifests at the appropriate time.

Please answer the following:

What is your Prayerful Intention?

_____

_____

_____

Is what you are doing now helping your intention?

_____
_____
_____

Have you said anything bad about your intention?

_____
_____
_____

Are you positive or negative toward your intention?

_____
_____
_____
_____
_____

Are you speaking affirmations about your intention? Are you re-minding yourself daily about your intention? Why or why not?

_____
_____
_____
_____
_____

What is coming out of your mouth about your intention or to-wards your intention?

_____
_____
_____
_____
_____

Yes, you know your intention, and you can recite it every day, but you must speak life about your intention, as well. You must speak positively about your intention. Even when it is hard, and you do not know if this is what you want anymore. You have to remember the Prayerful Intention you took the time to create with God and speak the truth that God said to you. That truth is you are Manifesting in Abundance. Therefore, no matter what things look like, you are going to manifest in Abundance. You have to say to yourself, "Self, God promised abundance, and that is what I expect." Practice:

What positive things can you say to yourself as you continue on this journey of Manifesting in Abundance?

_____
_____
_____

What positive prayers can you pray?

_____
_____
_____

What is your Prayerful Intention?

_____
_____
_____

Do you really believe you can Manifest in Abundance?

_____
_____
_____

If so, then say this: "God promised me abundance, and that is exactly what I expect." Now repeat that until you believe it until it resonates with you. Because God is honestly saying Let's Manifest in Abundance.

Beloved, it is essential for your intention that you believe you can have all you say, and that Abundance is genuinely on the way. Do not be afraid of Abundance. After all, God is right there with you. Say your Prayerful Intention, walk out the principles, and Manifest in Abundance, Beloved!!!!!

NOTE FROM THE AUTHOR

Thank you so much for taking the time to read and participate in this book. I truly pray that you Manifest in Abundance with every Prayerful Intention you have. Remember, these principles help no matter what Prayerful Intention you set, so please use them repeatedly. Remember to be in the moment, walk-in truth, walk with God, enjoy the moment, trust God without limits, have vision, and be careful what you say, for there is indeed power in the tongue. I wish you the best and pray for God's blessings and favor in your life.

Peace, Beloved.
Dr. Minniel Douglas
minniel@peacebeloved.co

DEFINITIONS AND GENERAL INFORMATION

Manifesting in Abundance: is overflowing and overly sufficient supply that is plain to see with the eyes and easily understood with the mind.

Medivotion: Meditation + Devotion. Medivotion is the place where meditation and devotion meet. It is a unique process that merges meditation and devotion. The goal of Medivotion is to relax and center yourself in the moment so that you can hear from God. It's about growing in relationship with God, gaining clarity of self and clarity of God. This leads to true authentic self and divine relationship so that you can love the Lord your God with all your heart, soul, and mind and love your neighbor as yourself. Therefore, the ultimate goal of Medivotion is the greatest commandments. You can find more information and book a session on peacebeloved.co

Life Coaching: is a series of sessions intended to help you reach a goal. A Life Coach may help you create a goal, whether in a career, relationship, business, or personal area of your life. Your Coach will also help you to create a plan to achieve this goal. The beauty of a Life Coach is he or she is there to support, encourage, and hold you accountable for your goals. Life Coaching is not therapy, though. It will not dig deep into the why's and how's of your being. Even with that, a Life Coach can help you manifest if you are willing to take the journey. Heads up, if you are interested in a Life Coach, Peace, Beloved does have that service available. Check it out at peacebeloved.co

ABOUT THE AUTHOR

Minniel Douglas

 Dr. Minniel Douglas loves people and lives to see them manifested into their best self. She holds a Medical Doctorate, is an Ordained and Licensed Minister, and a Certified Life Coach. She holds a Certification to practice Medivotion, Yoni Steaming, and Reiki. Upon her journey to know herself and God better, she developed the practice of Medivotion and opened Peace, Beloved (a safe place to grow in relationship with yourself and God). The journey also led her to walking out the 7 Principles of Manifesting in Abundance, and to the sharing of that revelation with you in this book.

Printed in the USA
CPSIA information can be obtained
at www.ICGtesting.com
CBHW052113070724
11266CB00009B/432

9 781736 687406